Backyard Bird Guide:
Attracting Wild Birds to Your Yard

By: Brian Grant

Published by:
Brian Grant and Random Technologies
4409 HOFFNER AVENUE, SUITE 347
Belle Isle, FL 32812

Table of Contents

Thank You for Purchasing this Book!

Visit the Site Below to Sign Up for Your
FREE UNADVERTISED BONUS

http://www.attractingwildbirds.com

1. Introduction

Many of us enjoy watching birds flit and flutter around our backyard. We may even fill bird feeders with seed, inviting them to nosh while we enjoy their beauty and flights of fancy. What many do not know or understand is the importance of backyard birding to birds and the environment that we share with our feathered friends.

As real estate development devours wildlife habitat, backyard birders have become vital to the survival and safety of birds. Planting trees and shrubs and providing nesting boxes are welcome mats for birds. You'll enjoy keeping a watch journal as you log the different species flocking to your backyard.

Throughout this book there are hints and tips for your backyard birding adventure. We'll discuss the types of birds to expect, how to attract different birds to your yard and when you can expect to see them. Near the end of the book, a guide to writing a journal is included so you may begin tracking your winged wayfarers. You'll feel joy, laugh and become attached to the birds that visit you.

The first section of this book outlines how you may experience backyard birding right away. In the second section, detailed directions and birding tips add to your enjoyment and enhance your birding knowledge. Section three describes the species to expect, along with instructions for writing in your log as you record your bird watching and backyard participation. We also discuss some of the most common birds frequenting North America, particularly the Eastern seaboard. While we mention bird types such as sparrows or finches, for more information on a particular species you're invited to visit your local library or contact the Audubon society in your area.

As you continue reading, you will soon find why people take interest in backyard birding. Watching birds is an interactive hobby. It's more than collecting pictures and field notes. It is a pastime that, when combined with journals and photos, gives you insight on seasonal changes in the weather and climate in your region. Birds are the first to feel the effects of a changing environment. If you pay attention to their habits and actions, you will begin to notice variations in the environment and climate around you, too.

As a novice birder, we suggest that you start with simple steps that provide for your birds. We don't want you to feel overwhelmed and then lose interest. We provide a learning arc as you progress so you'll want to entice even more birds to your yard. You'll gain a sense of accomplishment while providing your birds a more interactive and enjoyable experience.

Backyard birding is fun for all. Children learn to identify birds, watch their natural activities and even help with logging a journal and keeping their own chronicles. If we begin educating children and others on the benefits and rewards of backyard birding, the survivability of future birds can be insured. You'll find advice from any number of organizations and clubs on how to make your birding more satisfying. And you'll make new friends with whom you can share your experiences.

Beyond what we mention briefly here, there are many other books detailing individual species and ones dedicated specifically to backyard bird gardening. You'll even find books on how to attract specific birds to your yard. The local Audubon Society is the best place for resources on specific topics relating to birds.

When beginning your backyard birding adventure, remember to start slowly. Don't feel the need to add everything described in this book at once. Simple is the best way for both you and your feathered friends. By starting slowly, you will be able to gain confidence in your abilities and learn how to create a journal while gradually increasing your expertise. If you merely follow these general guidelines, you will find that backyard birding is an enjoyable, lifelong experience from which you, your family and your bird visitors will reap many rewards.

The following sections will lead you through the journey of backyard birding. The basics will serve as a stepping stone for you to advance into its more detailed aspects. You'll discover how birding influences the environment, your loved ones and you.

Figure 1. Yellow Warbler

2. What is Backyard Birding?

As we begin, let's explain the term "backyard birding." People may assume that to become a backyard birder you need a backyard. Nothing could be further from the truth. Backyard birding starts with the basics; adding a bird feeder, keeping a journal and contributing to the ecosystem by providing a sanctuary for birds. No matter if you live in a honeycombed apartment or on a sprawling ranch, you can be a backyard birder. If you enjoy your community's natural habitat, you can turn your visits into a backyard birding experience by keeping a journal and/or taking pictures of the birds you see. While this book is geared toward those who can maintain a backyard for birding, we offer many suggestions and helpful hints to guide you through the experience of becoming a backyard birder wherever you may live.

The best course of action when beginning your adventure in backyard birding is to start simple. Supply the basics: a bird feeder (preferably the hopper style; we will discuss the different types later), a simple birdbath with fresh water and some native plants. As you progress and become more familiar with birding, you can then progress to more lavish and detailed items for your backyard birds.

The journal you start will become an invaluable tool. You will be able to record the different species that visit your yard as well as time of year, weather conditions and type of activity. You will then begin to understand what you need as you decide and plan your backyard bird garden. You will also find that by watching you've seen many more birds then you first anticipated.

Backyard birding is simple to start but can become a passionate and enjoyable hobby. It's fun for the entire family -- everyone can participate. You can make a game for children as you spot birds while educating them on the finer qualities of bird watching. Create coloring books for youngsters to color different birds as an aid in identifying the different species of birds that visit. The activities you can do are endless. Many craft and hobby supply houses cater to the backyard birder.

3. Why Backyard Birding is Needed

Backyard birding is important for a variety of reasons. Conservation and understanding the ecosystem in our own backyard and the world as a whole imparts an increased awareness of our natural surroundings. Backyard birding offers many hours of enjoyment and beautifies your yard and home.

Until you immerse yourself in backyard birding, you may not realize its additional benefits. A prime consideration is conserving the ecosystem in your yard. Introducing plants and fauna not only improves your yard's appearance but invites wildlife to your doorstep. You'll learn, study and enjoy their presence. Real estate development deprives birds and humans of their natural surroundings so the backyard birder helps to maintain and restore balance to the ecosystem.

Figure 2. Eastern Phoebe Eating Insect

Birds help to control insect populations as well as keep the rodents at bay that destroy your garden and lawn. Without birds, mosquitoes and other pests would run rampant, leaving your yard and other natural areas in ruins. Imagine venturing outside and the first thing that greets you are swarms of annoying insects. Establishing your backyard birding area will help eliminate these scourges. A backyard birder enjoys fewer pests as well as a vast amount of birds that visit.

As you progress in your hobby of backyard birding, you will begin to add yard flowers and trees. As you do this, you increase a natural footprint and give back to nature. Plants and trees not only provide food and shelter to birds but increase oxygen levels in the air. They also reduce pollen content in the air and restore natural balance to your back yard.

These are not the only reasons to begin your backyard birding adventure. Many avian societies depend on the backyard birder to record notes on local species. This helps avian societies determine if a bird species is threatened or at risk. This information also gives information on the fitness of birds, their migration patterns and dietary habits. The backyard bird sanctuary is just that -- a sanctuary. Many rarely seen species are found in backyards.

Backyard birding is not limited to people who own yards and can cultivate a variety of plants. Anyone can be a backyard birder. People that live in apartments can add bird feeders or potted plants and small trees to their outdoor terrace to help attract birds. Small homes with limited yard space can do the same. A few simple feeders and a birdbath are sure to lure traveling birds and provide them an oasis in the middle of a sprawling urban development.

4. Attracting Wild Birds

Curious as to what types of birds you may see?

If you are like most, you notice robins, blue jays and an occasional cardinal. Once you begin the hobby of backyard birding you will be surprised how many more species you will notice and attract. Keeping a journal will help in identifying the many different species of birds visiting your yard, feeders and water sources. A hummingbird may visit and chickadees love the seed and plants put out for them.

The main species you attract to your back yard depends on the plants you have, types of seeds made available and water. Provide these basic requirements for birds and you'll be surprised at the many different types you will see. There are species of birds you may not have noticed; many birds passed up your yard before because some basics were missing. By following this guide you will soon discover a whole new world waiting for you to discover.

There are four basic requirements to attract more wild birds to your back yard. They are food, water, shelter and nesting areas. By providing these necessities in your back yard you will support many more species that will become regular visitors.

Food is the prime attraction that draws birds to your back yard. There are many different ways to present a pleasing offering to your feathered visitors. Bird feeders, native flora and garden plants all serve as enticements. Bird feeders are a great and inexpensive way to start. There are many different types on the market but as different birds have different needs some feeders may not attract those you desire.

Here are some basic types of feeders:

- The Platform Feeder, great for novice backyard birders
- The Tube Feeder
- The Hopper Feeder

Fresh, clean water is also very important. Plants provide safety, nesting and singing perches. You may provide water in a variety of different ways by using birdbaths, watering trays, ponds and misters.

You'll find different types of birdseed available commercially for use around your home. Fruits in the form of raisins and diced apples and oranges are popular choices. Seed bearing plants can be planted and harvested for storage. Commercially prepared products offer a wide variety from which to choose.

You can prepare hummingbird and oriole nectar in your kitchen with a simple mixture of sugar and water. Make sure the feeder you use has plenty of bright colors to attract the birds you want.

The types of species you attract will depend not only on the provender provided but your geographic location. Should you live in the northeast, do not expect to attract Eagles if you live on the seashore or plovers if you live in a city or where no water is available. Also, don't become discouraged during the first year. It often takes a second season for birds to become acclimated to the habitat you provide. If you start in late winter by preparing your backyard before birding season begins you will have a much better chance of success than if you started later in the spring.

Bird Feeders

Bird feeders range from a simple platform feeder to something more elaborate. Some feeders are built to look like an exact duplicate of the owner's home. Use your imagination and budget when choosing a bird feeder.

Be sure when you purchase a bird feeder to remember these simple points:

- It should be easy to clean
- The interior should be easily accessible
- Easy to fill
- Visually appealing

Birds are not particular to the appearance of a bird feeder, the food and cleanliness in and around the feeder is what matters.

The feeder you select will depend on your budget, size of yard and where it will be placed. Try not to purchase a feeder that overwhelms your yard or patio or is difficult to fill and clean. Begin with one that will help you enjoy your visiting birds and one that is not a chore to maintain.

Remember, you must enjoy what you provide or you could quickly lose interest.

The platform feeder is the simplest feeder to keep and maintain in your backyard. Filling it with seeds or fruit for a variety of different birds is effortless. The platform feeder is an open tray feeder available in a variety of sizes. It's also very simple to build. Consider adequate draining when buying or building a platform feeder; there should be a screen on the bottom that can be removed for easy cleaning and maintenance.

Figure 3. Platform Feeder

There should also be a raised rim for a perch and to keep the seed from spilling over. It should be large enough to accommodate a few birds at once. The feeder pictured above is a hanging style. However, other options include a freestanding feeder supported by a pole or feeders that can attach to your porch railing or a tree. You may use just about anything for a platform feeder from old birdbaths to used wooden chair seats. Your imagination is your only limit.

Hopper bird feeders are similar to platform feeders except they have a central hopper that holds birdseed and dispenses it as the tray is emptied. The hopper bird feeder is great for holding large amounts of food and any uneaten food is kept safe from bad weather because of its closed-in design. When shopping for a hopper-style bird feeder, look for these features that will make owning one easier and more enjoyable:

- Choose a large hopper with clear material, permitting birds to see their food and allows easy inspection so you know when to refill it
- You want one that is easy to fill, has multiple perches and feeding stations for your visitors
- One that holds various sizes of seeds

Figure 4. Hopper Feeder

Hopper style bird feeders come in many different sizes and shapes to compliment the decor of your garden. Be sure to find one you enjoy looking at as well as one birds find easy to use. You can use one or more styles, depending on the size and accessibility of your yard.

Another type of bird feeder that is easy to use and enjoyable for the novice is the tube style bird feeder. The tube style bird feeder is great for small birds like finches and small songbirds. Similar to the hopper style, these feeders are great in attracting the smallest of our feathered friends although you will find larger birds feeding at them from time to time.

Figure 5. Tube Feeder

While these bird feeders are perfect for the novice and expert backyard birder alike, there are also specialty types that will attract specific species of birds to your yard. The hummingbird feeder shown in figure five is a perfect example of these types of feeders and is sure to attract these elusive, but delightful creatures. Hummingbird feeders require a little extra care and maintenance; however, once you see "hummers" you will be fascinated by these little birds.

Figure 6. Hummingbird Feeder

Cleanliness is a very important point to remember about your bird feeders. Keeping the area free from spilled food not only keeps the area clean but prevents the spread of diseases. Regularly washing bird feeders will help keep them clean and prevent bacteria or mold buildup, which can spread diseases to both birds and humans. If you notice a feeder where the food has not been eaten then the feeder may be unclean, or contain bad food. It is best to discard the uneaten food properly and wash the feeder thoroughly. You can then refill it with the appropriate food for your avian visitors.

Bird Food

Birds rely on a variety of different foods to survive. You've taken the first step by providing bird feeders. Now you need to know what to put in them and other foods that you can plant in your yard for their enjoyment. While everyone knows birdseed attracts birds, there are specific types of seed that different birds prefer. For the novice, the commercially mixed type is the best choice until you establish a flock that frequently visits you. This type of seed is typically mixed with millet, milo, cracked corn, sunflower and nyjer seeds, along with other varieties that attracts birds to your feeder and yard.

If you want to attract larger birds, cracked corn works best as this is their typical food found in the wild. A favorite of songbirds is hulled sunflower seeds. These seeds contain essential nutrients and contain a high oil content to help your visitors maintain a healthy appearance. At the end of this book we've compiled a comprehensive list of birdseed specific to common bird species.

As mentioned earlier, commercial birdseed contains milo; while this is a cheaper type of feed, most backyard birds do not like it. Doves, pheasants and quail do enjoy this seed so if these are the birds you want to bring into your yard, milo will attract them. You may also see these birds under feeders picking up seeds dropped by birds at the feeders. Millet, another seed found both in the wild and in commercial seed is a favorite of small birds. Because this is a grass seed, it is a perfect complement to a dedicated bird garden in your yard.

Seeds are not the only food source that birds enjoy. Birds are efficient insect predators and find them anywhere from on the ground to in the air. They will help rid your yard of aphids, caterpillars and numerous other pests. A natural way to attract birds is to transform your yard into a bird friendly paradise. This is not to say that you should attract as many insects as possible; birds that visit your yard will find an abundance of insects without your help. Certain species are attracted to specific insects while others find no use for them.

There are other foods for birds besides those found in store-bought bags. You can grow many natural products in your backyard that will attract birds. Native trees and shrubs produce berries, fruits, flowers and seeds that attract wild birds. Crab apple and crepe myrtle trees are a favorite, especially during the cooler months when food starts to become scarce. It is best to plant shrubs and trees that are indigenous to your weather climate and region. Wild birds are accustomed to these native food sources and have been for hundreds of years.

When purchasing birdseed, keep in mind the type of feeder you have. Some seeds will not work in certain feeders due to the eating-hole sizes. Sunflower seeds will block the holes on many finch and chickadee feeders and are best suited for platform and hopper style feeders. On the other hand, finch foods are likely to pour through the bottom of a platform feeder. As an added safety measure, uneaten birdseed and seed that has fallen to the ground should be cleaned up regularly to prevent the growth and spread of avian diseases and bacteria as well as deterring the presence of unwanted rodents or other pests.

In sections two and three, we will detail what seeds and insects attract a specific species of bird. This will help you decide what types of seed you will want to add to your feeders. Do not limit yourself to attracting one single species. There will be many species that will still visit your feeders and yard but use the suggested feeds as a guideline for use of multiple feeders to attract birds to certain parts of your yard. You can also use the suggestions to attempt to lure new birds into your yard. Remember patience is the key to success in backyard birding.

Storing Bird Food Safely

Generally, only purchase enough bird feed for a short time but if you have bought in bulk there are different ways to safely store your excess seed. Always ensure your birdseed is fresh and appealing to birds. This means storing your bird feed in appropriate containers and being vigilant to the quality of your seed. Generally, birdseed packaging is not safe to use for long-term storage. Allow a week at most provided it is kept inside and not spilled. Spilt seed attracts rodents. Without taking proper precautions in storing your seed, you could soon have unwanted visitors in the form of mice or even rats.

Many backyard birders (including yours truly) perform best practices by storing seed in plastic or metal containers sealed with lids. These containers can be milk cartons for easy pouring into small and tube feeders. A larger container works well for filling hopper style feeders. These practices ensure that seed stays fresh, dry and away from rodents searching for food. When looking for containers to store your birdseed, look for types that are convenient to carry to your bird feeder without much trouble. Don't make it difficult to fill your feeders, especially if you have them placed around your yard or you must go great distances to fill them.

A yard pest that may look and act cute and funny can also be a problem: the raccoon. They can open anything and, given the opportunity, your birdseed containers. If birdseed is stored outside it will soon become a raccoon's favorite food. Remember, if you can open it, carry it or spill it, so can a raccoon. They have nimble paws adept at opening, spilling and carrying off your seed.

The best way to keep raccoons at bay is to store your seed in airtight containers and keep containers inside a shed or garage out of reach of the masked marauders. I know some birders that keep their seed in large metal garbage cans (they are serious backyard birders with a large amount of land and use seed rather quickly).

Having fresh, clean food for your birds is important to encourage repeat visits and to help maintain their health. Always check food supplies for dampness, bugs, mold or other growth that does not look right. Feed that has gone bad will cause serious health problems for sensitive birds -- you could wipe out an entire flock with just one feeding. Bacteria can grow quickly on seed stored improperly, potentially causing you considerable expense and waste. When buying new food, rotate your stock. Birdseed has a shelf life of just over a year when stored properly away from rodents, water and foul weather.

To recap, feed storage shouldn't be complicated or unhealthy to either birds or humans. Keep food in easily accessible and pourable plastic containers inside a storage shed or garage away from rodents and raccoons. Rotate your stock regularly and immediately dispose of any bad seed in a sealed plastic bag. Do not get rid of it in your yard, as this will only spread disease, invite rodents and allow bacteria to grow.

Water for your Birds

You have provided the food for your visitors, but another essential element for your feathered friends is fresh and clean water. Water is essential -- it provides not only a fresh drinking supply, but also an oasis for birds to preen, bathe and cool themselves, especially on hot summer days. Hummingbirds are known to fly back and forth in misters until dripping wet before going off to preen. You will find a variety of ways to provide water for the birds that frequent your backyard. Use one or choose many different methods; some no doubt will amuse you and entertain your bird friends.

Figure 7. Bird Bath

When supplying a watering source for birds, be sure to locate it where you are able to provide a constant fresh source of water. Fresh water is clean -- not stale or stagnant -- and reduces disease-carrying insects such as mosquitoes. A fresh water supply is important to the backyard birder because it provides a refuge and a water supply, especially during dry, hot summers.

Fresh water also allows birds to bathe and preen, removing unwanted parasites from their feathers. A large birdbath will quickly fill with birds during summer months when natural water supplies run low or become undrinkable, so keep it constantly full of clean water. A cooling mist will become a playground for birds that visit your backyard as they dart in and under the refreshing spray.

When looking to add a water source, you can choose the tried and true birdbath. Or you may add a pond to your yard or even a water mister. Keep in mind when supplying water to your backyard that water movement not only attracts more different species of birds than a bird feeder but also prevents water from becoming stagnant. If you are a beginner, it is recommended that you start with the birdbath available at many garden and landscape shops until you become better acquainted with backyard birding.

Ponds and waterfalls are not only great for bird habitats, they are also soothing and attractive adjuncts to your back yard. When designing your pond and waterfall, make sure you add items such as ground cover and native plants similar to the area surrounding the pond. Moss is a perfect ground cover in that it provides a lush green carpet as well as a place where ground birds will find food sources.

Figure 8. A Small Backyard Pond with Moving Water

A simple and easy way to provide moving water into your bird garden is the birdbath. The birdbath comes in many different shapes and sizes that will compliment your lifestyle. When looking for a birdbath, try to find one that includes a water pump. Not only will you have a birdbath but also a functioning fountain to enhance your yard. Here in the Northeast, some types of birdbaths come with helpful heaters that keep water warm and inviting during long, cold winters.

Another water source that is easy to set up and used either alone or with birdbaths is the mister. The mister provides a cooling and cleansing spray of fine water droplets that many birds, especially hummingbirds, find enjoyable. You should place the mister where birds will find plenty of perches available, allowing them to rest and play. Hummingbirds love misters and will spend plenty of time hovering in them.

Providing water for your feathered visitors is more than an attraction for the birds -- it is an environmental improvement to your yard. Water is necessary to bring in nature's pest hunters. Birds of different species hunt not only insects, but also the rodents and snakes that inhabit your yard. Some are not noticed by human eyes but are easily seen by the sharp eyesight of the birds. As we go further into the book, you'll see how to identify the types of birds you can expect to attract if you provide them with a suitable natural habitat.

5. Gardening for Backyard Birds

Gardening for birds in your backyard starts before you buy plants. There are many resources available to help you design your perfect habitat, but first visit your local zoo's native bird habitat area. These areas have been designed with just one thought in mind -- the well-being and happiness of wild birds. Notice how plants are layered as you would see in their natural habitat. Trees and plants provide birds' necessities, food and nesting. Backyard birding gardens usually do not incorporate a manicured lawn. You will want to provide a section that closely resembles their natural habitat by adding deadwood and stumps, weeds and local plants.

When you are designing and planting your backyard bird garden, there's no need to make your entire yard a natural habitat. A corner section will add the needed benefit to attract birds. Planting conifers and pine trees provides a warm and deep roosting area for your birds as well as berries in the winter.

When traveling in the northeastern part of America, you will notice that many homes have what are known as windbreaks. These are particularly noticeable where people have designed their yards to appeal to birds that visit the area. These windbreaks serve to block cold winter winds from blasting your home and they provide the perfect sanctuary for birds.

Figure 9. A Backyard Bird Garden Designed with Layers

When you begin your garden you are not only providing a sanctuary for birds and inviting new species to visit, but you are also contributing to the ecosystem. You want trees that provide a high canopy and plenty of shade. In the Northeast, sugar maples and American beech trees are an ideal choice. They are also native to the area and will attract more birds. The trees act as both a resting place and a nesting area.

You may be thinking that you have a beautiful green lawn and do not want to plant there. The "perfect" lawn that is completely green, covered in grass and must be mowed weekly, hides' environmental hazards that you may not have considered. There are fertilizer and toxic chemicals that seep into the environment, ground soil and water table under your yard. There is also the weekly cutting that uses the energy of gasoline engine lawnmowers, which contributes to air pollution. You also create unnecessary yard waste as you likely fill plastic bags with grass clippings that are sent to a landfill.

After the upper canopy trees are established, you will want to plant a lower layer of smaller trees. Hornbeam and fruit trees work great and provide the natural look and feel of the wild that birds prefer. Below these trees comes a layer of tall to mid-size shrubs, which provide sanctuary and food. Berry-producing shrubbery gives your birds natural food sources found in the wild.

Ground cover is essential to your backyard bird garden. Another favorite spot for small and large birds alike is ivy. Birds easily hide among the many branches these plants provide. A good ground cover will also provide your feathered friends another place to find their favorite natural foods: seeds and insects.

To find out what's best for your yard while maintaining a natural appearance, visit a local natural area such as a lake, pond or forest and carefully observe what you see. Mother Nature has naturally provided a garden incorporating everything we've discussed. The variations of trees, canopies, lower layers, shrubs and ground cover are all provided naturally. Bring a camera and take pictures. Try to model your yard, or a section of it, after your photos. By constructing this guise of nature you will attract many different species of birds to your yard.

You will want to add a section of deadwood, e.g., log home or a dead hedge, to provide a place for insects, frogs, and a sanctuary for small birds. These log homes and dead hedges will attract the necessary insects where backyard birds gather. They need not overwhelm your backyard and can even add an ambiance to your surroundings. They can be positioned in a far corner so as not to be an eyesore. An out-of-the way location also provides a sense of security to the smaller birds that will frequent the log home or dead hedge.

Figure 10. Dead Wood

6. Your Bird Journal

Keeping a bird journal can be as simple as writing down the species and keeping a tally of the birds that you see. On the other hand, you can make a more detailed journal, one that provides enough information to make the Audubon Society proud. Let's look at some of the data you can include when making a journal.

A simple journal can be any notebook that is convenient to carry and easy to write in. Basic information would include a picture if you want to take one, the location of the sighting, as well as the date and time. You may wish to add other observations such as bird nesting, building nests, feeding habits or other notes you find interesting.

This is the best basic type of information with which to start. After you gain experience in backyard birding, you will want to begin a more in-depth journal.

In your journal (I use a new composition notebook every year and find that they are easy to organize. If you mark your pages, you have a quick reference from prior years) you will want at least one picture of the bird you're putting on that page. In addition, you may want to list its common name but also the Latin or scientific name. This is an interesting way to learn the origins and history of a bird's name. Always include the date and if you want more detail, include the approximate time of your sighting. Don't forget to note weather conditions and the season. This is important especially when you look back across the years to notice patterns of the bird species you are observing and the time of year they visit, for migratory birds.

Your next entry line would be if the bird is solitary or with a flock. Details on a bird's actions, feeding, roosting and other observations should be added. If birds are in your yard, you will want take note if they are frequenting specific plants and trees.

The list is endless. In my journal, I have a section on a few special birds that kept returning year after year, especially a pair of hummingbirds and a blue jay. I note if they are together, any fledglings that are with them and their mates. As well as the dates they arrive and leave, what they eat and their overall condition.

With the ongoing impacts from climate-change, deforestation, lack of food and other challenges. It is important for humans to provide safe havens and stop-off points for traveling wild birds. Your helpful snacks and clean water supply will help insure the wild bird's survival.

7. Choosing Birdbaths, Birdhouses, and Feeders

In a previous section, we discussed the basics of birdbaths and bird feeders. Now let's go a little deeper and talk about how to choose what is right for your yard and what types of feed attracts specific birds.

Different types of feeders, baths and houses are species specific. Some birds will not flock to one type of feeder but will enjoy another. Different water sources and houses affect different species as well. Little birds may find it difficult using a birdbath that is too deep and they will quickly shy away from it. If you follow some of the guidelines below, you will have no trouble picking out the right birding supplies for your backyard garden.

When you choose a birdbath, take into consideration the many factors that will attract birds to your yard. Birdbaths should be designed with the bird in mind but should be pleasing to the eye of the gardener. Besides being functional, the birdbath should be easy to maintain.

You can choose from many different varieties -- hanging, pedestal, wall mounted, ornamental or plain. Choose something that you find appealing, is functional and fits your landscaping. Birds only look for the ease of water use and safety of access. If the water is too deep they will move away; if it is too shallow you will need to refill the bath more often, especially during hot weather.

Things to Consider When Choosing a Birdbath:

- Cost may be your first priority. You can spend as much or as little as you want. Remember, birds cannot read price tags -- they just want a place to drink and bathe.

- Size is the next consideration but it should not so small as to limit space just a few birds. If the smaller ones feel crowded they will use it sparingly. Moreover, larger birds will chase smaller species away.

- How your birdbath appears is very important. Pick one that you like. Remember, if you like the look of your birdbath then you will be more inclined to take better care of it.

- Make sure it fits your landscape design. Do not buy a birdbath that looks out of place. Choose something appropriate, as you do not want your bath to either overpower or become lost in your yard.

- The height of your birdbath is important to the type of birds that frequent your yard. Small birds like to be higher up for a sense of security and safety, while larger birds will drink from lower level or even ground level birdbaths, but insure it is in a safe location away from predator hiding places.

- Look for birdbaths that provide for the comfort of the birds. Small lips or perches work best for small birds so their feet have a place to grip while they drink. Water depth is also important for bird comfort. Provide depths ranging from 1 inch to 4 inches; the variation in depth allows drinking and preening.

- Look for birdbaths that are easy to clean. Baths with intricate details will harbor bacteria and become a hazard to the health of your birds.

- Finally, look for a birdbath that fits the climate where you live. Here in the Northeast, our winters can be long and cold. Thus, choose baths with heaters to prevent icing. Your winter flocks will appreciate the warm drink and visit more often.

When contemplating birdbaths consider adding more than one, especially if you have a roomy and large yard. By using different sizes and shapes with varying heights and styles you will attract more birds. You'll find that the variety of birds you attract will be visually appealing. Not only do multiple birdbaths attract more birds, you will also see birds that normally do not feed at a bird feeder. A backyard pond with flowers and flowing water is an added benefit to your yard. It provides an attractive addition that returns an ecological balance of flowing water to your backyard. Always remember to keep birdbaths and water fresh and clean.

Birdhouses are a favorite decoration for backyard bird watchers. In addition to being an aesthetic ornament they also provide safety and an ideal roosting and nesting place for birds that visit your yard. With the proper birdhouse you will be able to observe the nesting and mating habits of many species. As with birdbaths, functionality is as important as appearance. Keep in mind that birdhouses can be species specific, a lot depends on the entry-hole style of the house and the house's location in your yard.

When choosing houses for your birds, consider the types of birds you are trying to attract, the time of year you wish to put out your house and of course, your budget. Start simple for smaller birds and work your way up. Once you have mastered the basics and become familiar with caring for your birdhouse, you may graduate to larger, more elaborate and species-specific houses.

Figure 11. Blue Bird House

Birdhouses are like homes for humans: varying in design, built for different purposes and come in all sizes, shapes and styles.

However, by following some basic steps you will take the mystery out of buying or building a birdhouse for your backyard. One important feature is the ease of opening the birdhouse for cleaning purposes. You will discover birdhouses that are species specific. Some birdhouses with perches are not compatible for finches or bluebirds because it permits easy access by predators. In this chapter, you will find descriptions of the types of birdhouses that you can use for certain species that also meets their needs.

There are three different types of birdhouses that are species-specific. You can build or buy these birdhouses for your yard by shopping at a local garden center or landscaper. These birdhouses are:

- Bluebird
- Purple Martin
- Finch

Each birdhouse is designed to protect the nesting birds of the species listed. Although other species may take up residence in the houses, these are the three main nesting birds that will visit your backyard, especially during the winter.

Birdhouses can be obtained in many ways: you can buy them from your local hardware store or landscape shop, or, if you are handy with tools, you can build your own. There are also artisans that specialize in building birdhouses.

Birdhouses protect a nesting bird from natural and unnatural predators, provide a nesting place during the breeding season and give sanctuary to birds during foul weather. By following these suggestions, you will provide a safe environment for your bird friends. You can follow them through their life cycle from breeding, mating and birth to their yearly migration.

By having birdhouses in your backyard, you will gain the knowledge of how birds migrate, maintain a 'family structure' and if you keep a journal of your sightings, be able to provide and help local and national bird associations with important wild bird data.

There are only a few basic requirements to follow should you decide to build a birdhouse. First, never use pressure treated wood. The chemicals in this wood are harmful to the bird, environment and humans. The inside of the birdhouse should be left natural with no paint or sealer, as these are toxic to hatchlings and mature birds alike.

Always make sure you can easily clean out your birdhouse. Adding a latched door to the bottom makes cleaning easy. Many hobby stores, garden shops and landscape shops sell birdhouse plans and kits to help with your project.

Bluebird Houses

Due to increased development in rural areas, many nesting birds require humans to provide the material and safety of a nesting box for their continued survival. Man-made nesting boxes are ideal for bluebirds as long as they're made from a natural wood like cedar or redwood. The wood inside the nesting box must remain in its natural state, as most paints are toxic to birds and their fledglings. Boxes can be painted on the outside, but use light colored, non-toxic paints, as bluebirds tend to shy from extremely bright and flashy colors.

Your bluebird birdhouse should have a floor size of about 5" x 5" with a one and three-quarter inch entry hole and be between eight and twelve inches tall. The box should be easily accessible; it should be able to be opened from top, bottom or front for easier cleaning. Also, the bottom of the box should have drainage holes as sitting water will cause bacteria to grow.

A bluebird house needs ventilation at the top of the house with holes on all sides. In addition, do not provide perches on the house; predators will find easy access with a perch. Add roof overhangs that extend at least 2" – 5" to stop cats, squirrels and raccoons from reaching into the box. The locations where you mount your bluebird box is very important to the safety and comfort of the bluebirds use it. Place your box on a tall pole or fence post within 100 feet of trees or shrubs. This is for the safety of the young as they leave the house since they will want to fly directly to a safe perch.

When installing bluebird houses always position them in pairs. This is because sparrows may take up residence in one box while leaving the empty one for bluebirds to nest. Pine needles and soft grasses are the preferred nesting material of bluebirds so be sure to have these near the birdhouse.

Cleaning out the bluebird houses is important but only after the bluebirds have left the house and nesting season is over. Use a mixture of 1:4 parts bleach and water to clean the inside of the house. Remove and discard old nesting material in an appropriate trash container. Do not leave it on the ground as this will promote bacteria and spread diseases.

When bluebirds look for a suitable nesting area, the male first finds a spot and brings nesting material to it in hopes of attracting a female. Once the female approves of the nesting box, she will begin building the nest to prepare for the eggs. By following the simple details provided, you should be able to attract and enjoy the antics of a pair of nesting bluebirds for many years.

Purple Martin Houses

When you see a purple martin birdhouse, you will notice that they look nothing like any other birdhouse you have seen. Unlike most other birds, purple martins like human activity around the area where their birdhouses are located. They are also the only bird that requires humans to provide their housing during mating season. They have very specific size and placement needs. Purple martin houses also need to be painted a bright white to reflect the bright sunlight and keep the houses cool during the hot months.

Figure 12. Purple Martin House

Purple martin houses should have a floor space of about 7" – 7" or larger and can be made of almost any material except pressure treated wood. You will also want to mount your birdhouse from twelve to twenty feet off the ground and have a way to raise and lower it for cleaning. You will want to supply pole guards to prevent snakes, cats and other predators from climbing the pole to get at the birds.

Purple martins are very particular about having a completely unobstructed flight path to their boxes. No trees should be near their boxes as the purple martin likes to fly in a straight path towards their nests from a minimum of 60 feet in any given direction. There should be no trees within 40 feet of your purple martin housing and no trees higher than that of their houses. You may place the boxes closer to trees should the houses be taller. Provide a minimum of at least 24 nesting boxes. This will provide a good colony for your purple martins.

To provide a safe haven for your birds, do not have bushes or shrubs near the base of the houses and never attach wires to the poles. Martins fly fast; wires will become an obstruction that could possibly injure the martins as they swoop and dive around their houses. You need to take down the houses after the season is over. The purple martin is a migratory bird and comes to the United States to nest so in late fall or winter the owner of the houses should prepare their housing for the purple martin's next arrival.

For cleaning and maintenance, purple martin houses are best mounted on a flagpole so that you can easily raise and lower the houses. By doing this you will be able to take down the nesting boxes when the nesting season ends and prevent unwanted birds from taking up residence in the boxes. Note that unmonitored Purple Martin houses are often claimed by more aggressive, non-native species such as European starlings.

Finch Houses

Finches are among the most popular and frequent visitors to your backyard. They come in all shapes, colors and sizes although small compared to the typical backyard bird. You will find the typical finch birdhouse as a 6" – 6" floor area with a perch at the entrance hole that is cut to around one and one-half inches round.

Figure 13. Finch House

Finch birdhouses are best mounted out of reach of predators common to yards. The hole for finches should be small; anything over one and a half inches would be too big. A larger entry hole would invite competition from house sparrows who would evict the finches. As with other birdhouses, wood is the best material. While it should be natural and untreated on the inside the exterior can be as elaborate as your imagination.

Some people even construct their finch birdhouses as a miniature model of their residence. As with all birdhouses, keeping the house clean is important to attract finches to your backyard. Most finch houses should have a removable top or sides for easy cleaning and to allow access to check on the nesting brood. When cleaning out your birdhouse, always dispose old nesting material in a garbage receptacle. Discarding on the ground will invite unwanted bacterial growth and spread diseases throughout your birding community.

Bird feeders

As we discussed earlier, bird feeders vary and are only limited by imagination and budget. Some birds however require specific types. The hummingbird, a small, brightly colored bird, is a nectar and small insect eater. Hummingbird feeders are designed to hold a sugar water solution that hummers love. The design allows their long beaks to sip the nectar from the provided holes provided and prevents nectar from spilling out.

Figure 14. Hummingbird Feeder

It's best to make your own hummingbird nectar. Commercial powder and liquid food contains toxic chemicals harmful to birds. Boiling a solution of 1:4 parts sugar and water, then cooled, makes perfect nectar for the hummingbird.

Hang your hummingbird feeder so that ants cannot easily get to it. It's also important to keep the area clean as the feeder will quickly become popular with bees and other nectar-feeding insects. Other visitors to the hummingbird feeder are orioles, woodpeckers and nectar drinking bats.

A hummingbird feeder can be kept up year round for the occasional oriole that ventures into your yard. When cold weather arrives, bring the feeder inside every evening to prevent the solution from freezing.

Careful attention must be paid to the food, as hot temperatures will soon cause the sugar-water mixture to go bad. The solution can become moldy if not changed or checked daily. It is best to start with a small amount of food in your feeders. By doing this you can monitor use and increase food supply as needed.

Suet Feeders

Suet is a favorite food among many backyard birds and provides them a source of high calorie energy. Bird suet is a combination of hard fat mixed with birdseed such as grains, nuts and fruit. By adding a suet feeder to your backyard, you can attract an even more diverse species of birds such as woodpeckers, bluebirds and northern cardinals. While not essential, the suet feeder is an excellent addition to your feeders and provides a perfect protein supplement for winter birds.

Figure 15. Pine Warbler Eating Suet

Suet can be offered in a few ways but specialized feeders have been designed for ease of use. The cage feeder is the best option for holding suet cakes as it lets the birds hold on to the wire mesh while getting to the food. Some cage feeders also have a tail prop which allows bigger birds such as woodpeckers to feed with ease.

In addition to the cage feeder, there are also the log and the bag feeders. The log feeder allows you to add plug suet into pre-drilled holes. The log feeder helps to keep the suet dry and provides a natural feeding station for the birds. Bag feeders are hanging mesh bags filled with suet that can be used for any style of suet including plug, cake or even shavings. The only downside to the mesh bag feeder is that larger birds will not be able to use it. Small suet loving birds will have no problems.

When using suet as a staple for your birds, you need to take a few precautions. Certain suet types will melt in direct sunlight and on hot days. To prevent melting, only provide suet during the cooler months or place it in shaded areas to avoid direct sunlight. Note that suet with animal fat can become rancid quickly during hot summer months. Only offer enough suet that can be eaten within a day or two or place outside during sunrise and sunset hours of the day.

Suet is also a favorite of bullying birds such as the European starling. To prevent starlings from devouring the suet before the other birds have a chance, consider purchasing an upside down suet feeder and one with wire mesh designed to keep out larger birds.

Another concern with suet feeders is the presence of rodents and other pests. Mice, raccoons, squirrels and bears are quickly drawn to suet if left outdoors overnight. Move suet indoors during the evening hours to prevent unwanted guests from getting to the uneaten portion.

8. Sleeping Habits of Birds

One question that is often asked by new backyard birders: Where do birds go to sleep at night?

The answer varies by species, the amount of predators that inhabit the area and weather. Most birds sleep where their territory is. They usually sleep in short bursts, aware of predators that pose a danger to them. Some birds, such as the hummingbird, enter into a state of inactivity during the night, lowering their metabolism while they sleep in order to survive the long period without food.

Most birds will sleep on tree branches while some will rest on the ground or in woodpiles and shrubs. They prefer primarily higher locations away from light, noise and ground predators like cats and snakes.

The swift has a very unusual way to sleep. It is presumed that they actually sleep during flight, facing prevailing winds so they can remain aloft while sleeping. Some birds sleep with one eye open for constant lookout of predators. Most birds during winter months sleep in large flocks to stay warm with sentries protecting those asleep.

One thing is certain -- birds do sleep but have adopted the unusual ability of sleeping in very short bursts. They have the ability to sleep with one hemisphere of their brain on constant alert while the other rests. To understand the sleeping habits of the birds that visit your yard, observe them closely, especially when dusk approaches.

Noise and light pollution dramatically impact birds, as it does humans. However, birds do not have houses to shut out these disturbances. You can help by keeping bright lights away from trees or where you know birds sleep. Also, keep noise levels down after sunset. Take consideration of the birds that sleep from sunset to sunrise, they have enough unnatural sounds (airplanes, cars, trains, construction) to try and filter out.

Figure 16. Birds Sleeping at Night

9. Natural Foods and Habitat of Backyard Birds

There are a variety of ways to offer food to birds that frequent your backyard. These foods and seeds are provided by trees, shrubs and even weeds that grow in your yard. Although you still offer your avian visitors seed in feeders, it is a good conservation practice to provide native wild fruits, berries, and seeds from trees that you can plant and grow in your yard. The importance of trees is often overlooked. Not only do they provide shade to your home (which helps to lower household cooling costs), trees also provide necessities for birds: shelter and food.

Trees and Plants

Figure 17. Trees and Plants Garden

Trees and plants are an important and integral part of your yard. If your yard does not have trees, we suggest that you plant at least a few of them.

If you live in an apartment, trees in pots remain small but still offer your feathered friends a place to roost on your balcony. After the tree gains size and starts to outgrow the pot, you can contribute to your neighborhood by planting the tree in a park.

Some plants that you and your birds will enjoy are sunflower, thistle and millet plants. They provide important seeds and nutrients for birds and add attractive flowers to your yard. These seed-bearing plants are a favorite of finches, cardinals and other seed eating birds.

Planting a sunflower garden is both a simple and economical way to provide seed to your birds and yourself. They add a bright yellow color to your yard, enticing seed lovers to visit. Honeysuckle bushes and hostas attract hummingbirds and orioles, who also love red flowering plants such as the bleeding heart shrub, which produces a delectable nectar they crave. Another favorite of nectar hunting birds is the hollycock. The red and pink blooms are an enticement these birds can't resist. Hollycock makes an excellent border plant for your backyard bird garden.

Figure 18. Sunflowers

Planting and growing a backyard bird garden will benefit both you and your visiting birds. Some simple tips to guide you are provided here. You can gain more information by visiting your local landscape and gardening center. Use as many indigenous trees and flora as possible. Native plants and trees flourish in their local climate, thriving where many imports won't.

Trees are a particular benefit to both human and birds. Besides saving home energy costs from the shade they provide, trees also help to restore the habitat that once flourished in your area. Depending on species, you may consider adding native ornamental and flowering trees to enhance the beauty of your yard. Your local landscaping store can provide you with complete information on both native and non-native flowering and ornamental plants that grow in your climate zone. It is always best to plant local and native plants to your region, this provides a familiar source of food to birds and blends naturally with the surrounding landscape.

Plant tall trees in the back and on the north side of your garden to block wind and snow during the winter months. The best trees for this purpose are large pines as they stay green year round and provide cone seeds for larger birds. You want trees that offer a safe haven for birds to escape predators, provide space for nests in the summer and provide seed and sap for food. A mixture of deciduous and coniferous trees provide year round color and protection for birds and humans alike.

Similarly, trees native to the Northeast such as maple and birch trees provide a tall canopy many larger birds seek when roosting and nesting. You can find specific trees native to your region by taking a walk in a nearby forest. As you walk through the area, consider starting your birding journal on what you may want to include and how to keep records. When you return to look for trees to purchase, you will have a much better idea of what you want in your yard and what species of birds you can expect to attract.

Smaller trees planted near larger ones add a lower layer cover and are generally berry or fruit producing trees. Crepe Myrtles, popular in the Northeast, give a beautiful color display from spring to midsummer and their flowers produce nectar and pollen for birds and the insects that they feed on. During the fall and winter, they provide seed and perches for birds such as robins and cardinals as well as nesting areas for smaller birds seeking roosts in the late summer and early fall months.

Moving down from trees are the tall shrubs. These plants give birds the protection, berries and seeds they seek, all in the context of a natural setting. Tall shrubs are beneficial to both bird and homeowner as they act as a refuge for birds while promoting privacy and serving as a wind block for your yard.

Mid and large size shrubs are also beneficial to both birds and your yard. Many work well as wind blocking shrubs and will keep your yard dry from flooding after heavy rains. The buttonbush is a perfect example of this as it readily soaks up water from the ground. It also has plentiful fruits robins and blue jays love.

Low shrubs generally grow to 8' in height and offer birds hiding places from predators. These bushes also produce a fruit that is prized by robins during late afternoon feedings. Ground birds enjoy the fallen seeds and uneaten fruit. Low growing deciduous shrubs will bring birds to your backyard not normally seen at feeders. Waxwings and grosbeaks that typically do not come to bird feeders will enjoy these shrubs. You will enjoy watching these beautiful birds in their natural habitat. Low shrubs also provides cover and protection to ground nesting birds such as doves and pigeons and allows them to enjoy fruits and seeds without exposing themselves to typical backyard predators.

When looking for plants, shrubs and trees for your yard, stick with plants that are local to the climate zone where you live. This will give your yard a more natural look while providing birds with a familiar habitat. In addition, plants native to your area are much easier to maintain and will not become invasive to your natural yard. Always check with your local landscape store for more information and details about plants best suited for your area.

Figure 19. Desert Garden

10. Gardening and Pesticides

After you have designed and planted your garden, you will want it to flourish. Many people use pesticides and other fertilizers to bring a lush look to their yards and keep bugs away. Using these products is harmful to birds, your yard and the environment.

Pesticides and fertilizers contain toxins that quickly break down and enter the soil and water. When beginning your garden, use organic fertilizers that provide the proper nutrients needed for a beautiful garden. Pesticides are bad for everyone, especially wildlife.

If you provide the proper necessities required for birds and other wildlife, the use of pesticides is not needed. Nature's balance will bring insects under control, as birds will quickly make meals of them.

While some pesticides and fertilizers have an immediate impact on natural balance, some effects are not readily seen. Some pesticides are carried back to the nests where they are ingested by small hatchlings. The effects can range from immediate death to sterility and deformities. In addition, birds that ingest pesticides can move into different areas before dying. The upshot is that pesticides spread far beyond the original area of application as wildlife or domesticated animals ingest the toxins found in dead birds.

As you can see, there is a detrimental snowball effect; all parts of the ecological system become adversely impacted by the use of pesticides or fertilizers. By attracting natural wildlife, such as birds, there will be no need for pesticides and fertilizers in your yard. You will maintain both a verdant yard and a healthy bird population.

Many homeowners use pesticides to control the gypsy moth. These moths build huge nests that quickly overpower plants and trees. A natural way to deter these pests is to attract species that eat these pests, thereby destroying the gypsy moth colony. Blue jays, chickadees, woodpeckers, orioles and robins all happily feast on gypsy moths. If you attract these birds to your yard they will aid in destroying these pests in a natural and pesticide-free way.

Figure 20. Gypsy Moth

Instead of using a commercial fertilizer, consider using organic alternatives that won't add toxins to your lawn. Good compost raked in and spread evenly will provide nutrients to your lawn and give your yard a lush look without damaging the fragile ecosystem and bird and wildlife populations.

When caring for your yard you have many alternatives from which to choose. By researching natural and organic alternatives, you'll find environmentally friendly products to grow a verdant lawn without damaging the ecosystem. Another safe option to keep your lawn green is to create your own natural compost fertilizer.

Remember, Mother Nature doesn't use chemicals, toxins or fertilizers. She works naturally, which is a lesson we can all take to heart.

Figure 21. Compost Bin

11. Predators

North American birds have many predators, ranging from other birds to domesticated and feral cats. Some predators are not after the bird but rather their food found in feeders and their eggs in nests.

Squirrels are notorious for damaging and eating your expensive bird food. They also chew holes into a bird feeder to access the food. You can combat this by making or buying squirrel-proof accessories for your feeders. These squirrel-proof deterrents can be simple baffles that prevent the squirrel from climbing directly to the feeder or nesting box. Remember this when squirrel-proofing anything: squirrels are very resourceful. They will perform extreme acrobatics in order to obtain their prize.

A natural predator of most birds is the hawk. The hawk will soar hundreds of yards above in the sky, looking for its prey -- typically slow moving, ground feeding birds. There are not many ways to deter hawks from hunting; this is their natural instinct. One strategy to keep them out of your yard is to close down your bird feeders for the winter season. However, this causes your smaller songbirds to move on, sometimes never to return. Predatory birds are not too much a concern, as they were built and designed to eat smaller birds, so you may see: eagles, hawks, kestrels in your bird habitat. Bringing a whole new variety of feathered companions into your yard.

House and feral cats pose the greatest risk to backyard birds. Recent studies show that up to 3.7 billion wild birds are killed each year by cats. While some deterrents work, such as: remove or covering food sources from trash bins, scattering orange or lemon peels or applying citronella oils to the areas you find where cats visit will help, but realize that most will not. Adding a bell to a pet cat's collar will work until the cat learns to move without ringing the bell. Their favorite tactic is to ambush ground feeding birds under feeders and shrubs. The best way to prevent cats from killing birds is to keep them indoors at all times, if you are a cat owner. This is the only foolproof way, especially since a cat's natural instinct is to hunt prey such as birds. Undoubtedly house cats provide the greatest danger to backyard birds. Feral cats that hunt in packs can quickly devastate a population of local birds, driving them from the area or wiping out the bird population entirely. Contact your local animal control to help with a feral cat problem; they will trap and remove them. Controlling your own domesticated cat will aid in maintaining the bird population and reduce predation.

Figure 22. Cat

Another predator of birds is rodents (mice and rats). Rodents are attracted to the seed droppings underneath most feeders. Thus, it is of utmost importance to keep this area clean. Rodents not only eat seeds but will attempt to destroy the nests of ground birds if a rodent colony becomes established. Rodents often carry diseases and this can spread quickly to a bird population if left unchecked. You can prevent some or most of the seeds from hitting the ground by building a catch basin to hold the dropped seeds. Note that catch basins need frequent cleaning since bird droppings can contaminate seeds with salmonella.

Squirrels are another predator of birds. Squirrels will take birds' food and even try to get into the nests and remove eggs. With a little ingenuity you can squirrel-proof your bird feeders and nests. Start with basics such as squirrel rings around tree trunks and poles. Put tubes around wires that squirrels use to climb to a feeder hung in the middle of your yard. Unfortunately, squirrels are an adaptable and resourceful pest. For every obstacle you place in their path, they will try to find a way to overcome it. It is no exaggeration in saying that outsmarting squirrels is a full time job.

The squirrel's partner in crime when it comes to the destruction of bird habitat is the raccoon. These formidable predators are infamous for reaching inside nesting boxes and removing eggs and hatchlings. They will also try to get at birdseed by climbing poles or moving across lines. To deter raccoons, use strategies similar to the ones you use against squirrels. Erect guards that prevent them from reaching bird nests. Also make sure to keep feeding areas clean and free from rubbish, as seeds will attract raccoons.

Snakes are another predator but they play an important part in the ecosystem of the food chain. If you find a snake, do not kill it; if possible, catch and release it in another area. To prevent snakes from entering your nesting boxes, install the boxes on a metal pole or apply hot sauce to the pole. Hot sauce does not affect birds (they have been known to eat chili pepper seeds) but it does deter most mammals since they do not like the taste of the fiery liquid.

House sparrows and starlings are an invasive species not protected by any law. These birds will easily kill any nesting birds or their hatchlings, destroy nesting boxes, and drive out the local bird population. By law, you are allowed to destroy their nests in an effort to deter them from taking up residence on your property. Early intervention of this species is necessary as they can quickly overrun your native songbirds and their habitat in your yard. House sparrows and starlings also devastate the local ecosystem. First introduced to North America from Europe, they quickly overran local bird populations. House sparrows and starlings will eat natural seeds and destroy your home's garden. The best strategy is to scare off these predators before they take up residence on your property.

We would be silly if we did not mention dogs. They will attack nestlings, ground feeders and if they can reach the nesting box, the hatchlings. To prevent dogs from becoming a serious predator, keep them away from the areas where birds are nesting and during the season when most fledglings begin to take flight, usually between July and November. Keep your dog on a leash to prevent them from attacking wildlife. Just one bite from a dog invariably proves fatal to any bird. Walking your dog is a healthy way for both you and your pet to experience nature as you stroll through the woods. Use a leash to keep both your pet and the local wildlife safe.

Figure 23. Predators

12. Bird Migration

Before we discuss regional birds, let's mention terms like migration and migratory paths. Bird migration varies from species to species. Not all backyard birds migrate; they will remain within an area year round. These are sedentary birds such as chickadees, blue jays and robins. The migration of birds follows a regular seasonal pattern. With the onset of cooler or warmer weather; most migratory birds begin to form flocks to prepare for their journey.

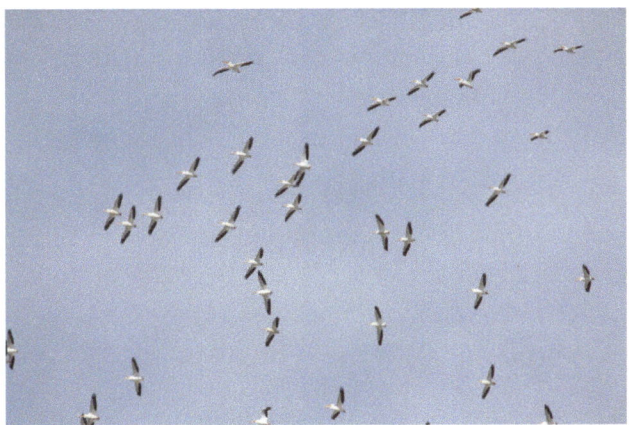

Figure 24. Birds Migrating

The causes of migration range from weather changes, habitat loss and lack of food. When birds do migrate, they generally travel in flocks. These flocks can range in size from a few hundred to a thousand or more. During the migration season, your backyard may become a temporary home to hundreds of birds looking to rest. Hence, your feeders and water sources will become depleted quickly and need to be refilled often.

Most migrating birds follow a path known as flyways. They take this same route, typically over land, year after year. Very few Northeast birds except for the purple martin migrate over water because of the lack of resting areas. Some migrations are merely short trips from higher to lower altitudes while others are longer journeys spanning thousands of miles from cooler northern latitudes to warmer southern climates.

By knowing the migratory times, you can prepare your backyard prior to the arrival of your birds. Purple martins send scouts ahead of the main flock, typically around March, and if everything is ready you may find Martins nesting in your backyard houses by the beginning of spring. By studying the migratory patterns of the birds that frequent your yard, you will become adept at forecasting seasonal changes. You'll be able to predict the approach of spring or the onset of a cold winter. Once you begin studying birds closely you'll discern climatological information gleaned from their activities.

Migrations are part of birds' genetic programming. Backyard birds of the Northeast follow these patterns like clockwork with minor variations due to food and habitat changes. If you have kept a journal, you will be able to estimate the arrival of the migratory birds in your area.

When birds begin to migrate their food requirements change. They will begin to eat more to increase their metabolism for the journey. You will also notice that many birds will begin to molt. That is to say that they replace old feathers with new plumage. This typically occurs to all migrating birds and is no cause for alarm.

Congratulations! You've now taken the first steps toward becoming a backyard birder. To help in the progression of your new pastime, we will list the different species you will see frequently and those that only visit during a particular time of the year. By learning to identify birds and understanding what they like, you will not only experience the joy of birding but learn how to keep them coming back year after year.

You will find that there is more than meets the eye once you establish feeders, plants and water sources in your backyard. You may soon have visits from the smallest of hummingbirds to the biggest of local birds, the eagle. I have one that visits my yard on a weekly basis.

Figure 25. Birds Migrating

13. The Bird Species

Birds are a diverse and enormous group consisting of warm-blooded vertebrates with feathers and wings that lay hard-shelled eggs. Their hollow bones enable flight. They have a four-chambered heart and an extremely high metabolism rate that allows them to survive in almost any environment.

Birds are considered a social species, even those that prefer to live solitary lives. They use calls and songs, color, and movement to communicate with other birds. While discussing the complete genus and evolution of birds is beyond the scope of this book, by mentioning various species we allow you to understand the workings and habits of birds.

There are more than 10,000 species of birds alive today ranging in size from a mere two inches (the bumblebee hummingbird) to nine feet tall (the ostrich). Birds are found from the Arctic to the Antarctic. In the northeastern part of the United States where this book focuses, 750 different species call the region home.

All birds bathe. The most common techniques used by birds in the Northeast is dipping and darting. These birds will dip themselves in water and splash water onto their backs. Darting birds will quickly dart into water, wetting their tail feathers and then flicking the water onto their back. If you have set up a birdbath in your backyard garden, you will be able to observe the many different ways that birds use these techniques. Birds bathe to keep their plumage in good condition and remove small dust particles picked up during foraging and roosting.

The social structure of birds is not as complicated as one might think. Most birds are social in nature and develop close-knit family groups.

The majority of birds found in the Northeast are monogamous in nature, usually remaining with their mate or life partner until one dies. This relationship promotes the survivability of the young since both parents protect the nesting site.

The ecological importance of birds cannot be overstated. Some birds play an important role in pollinating plants and flowers. The hummingbird is a good example; they have been observed with pollen covering their beaks and feathers as they move from plant to plant. Birds, particularly ground feeders, play a role in seed distribution. They pick up seeds, in their beaks or trapped in their feathers, and transport them to another destination, which allows plants to grow in a new area.

Nest building is as diverse as the birds themselves. Each species has developed a unique way to construct their nests. With time and observation, you will be able to identify a species by their nests. Most nests are made of natural material found locally. Some nests are tightly built resembling deep cones while others are simple structures with concave centers. Most nests are used only once by a species and a new one is built for each brood. This is why it is important to clean the nesting boxes or houses after each season as many will not return to a used nest. Some bird nests of the Northeast are constructed on the ground. These are usually of the quail, pheasant and sparrow genus. If you do have ground-dwelling birds around, take extra care with their safety from predators such as feral cats.

Humans cause the biggest problems facing birds. The massive decline of bird populations is due to the loss of their natural habitat caused by urbanization and land development. As recently as 2009, Bird Wildlife International recorded a decline in over 1,200 species. With this downturn, the role of the backyard birder is vitally important in making a productive impact on the environment and helping their feathered friends survive.

By eliminating the use of pesticides and inorganic fertilizers, the backyard birder can make a positive difference in their local ecosystem. While at first this may seem a quixotic task, understand that each individual contributes a part to protect wild avian species. As you begin your adventure into the world of backyard birding, you will acquire knowledge of not only the birds that you encounter but the delicate balance of the ecosystem that both humans and birds share. It is up to the backyard birder to provide a habitat that allows birds to survive while removing the toxins we have unwittingly introduced into the environment.

Below is a generalized list of birds that frequent the backyards of the northeastern United States. While this is far from exhaustive, for the beginner this list represents species you will likely see. As you grow more comfortable as a backyard birder, you will recognize more species and be able to address their basic needs -- food, water, shelter and nesting. Never underestimate the positive impact a backyard birder can have on the avian population.

Most of the birds listed are year round residents as only a few species in the Northeast are true migratory birds. As stated earlier, when a resident bird migrates, environmental influences play a large part. These include sudden climate changes and especially loss or reduction of food or habitat. By observing these patterns you will be able to adjust your feeding and backyard habitat to continue to please your visitors.

Cardinals

Figure 26. Male and Female Cardinal

Cardinals are a frequent and year-round resident of the Northeast. You will find them in your backyard if you provide the proper food and cover for them. One of the songbirds, its name comes from its brilliant red color and the Catholic clerics who wear distinctive red robes. A mid-size bird averaging around seven to eight inches with a wingspan between nine and twelve inches, the male is slightly larger than the female and much more colorful. The female, though lacking vibrant red color, is still a visually striking bird and an enjoyment to watch. Both sexes of the cardinal have face masks; the male sports a vivid black while the female's mask is usually grayer in color.

The Northern cardinal ranges from the lower regions of Canada to the upper half of Mexico. This bird is found in almost any habitat, from woodlands and gardens to shrub lands and swamps. Considered a non-migratory or resident bird, most cardinals tend to remain in one area unless there is a shortage of food or shelter.

The diet of the Northern cardinal consists mainly of weed seeds and grains. It also likes fruits and insects. For protein, the main staple of young cardinals is insects. The cardinal is generally a ground feeder, eating fruits and seeds dropped from trees. It will also scavenge insects found on the ground including beetles, snails and grasshoppers.

A favorite food for cardinals is sunflower seeds -- if you wish to see cardinals during winter, provide them with a hopper-style feeder filled with sunflower seeds. A suet feeder will also draw their attention as well as a source to provide them with protein they need for winter months.

Cardinals mate for life. They will remain together all year round -- feeding, hunting and mating together. The male helps the female in nest building by bringing her material but the female is the primary nest builder. The nest is used only once; the next season they will construct a new one. Each nest contains on average three to four eggs with the female doing the incubating while the male brings her food. In ten to twelve days the eggs are hatched and the male begins to take care of them as the female starts to incubate another clutch of eggs. Cardinals can have from three to four broods per year.

The cardinal is a songbird territorial in nature. Their songs are crisp and clear sounding, similar to a whistle. The male will chase away any other male that does not acknowledge his songs and will defend his territory and mate. The song of the cardinal varies from region to region and can be quickly distinguished from other cardinals in the area. The cardinal will use its song to locate its mate when night is near or visibility grows dim.

The territorial male cardinal will fight any male that enters its territory. It has even been known to put up a ferocious fight with its own reflection in a glass or a mirror until it tires itself out or the reflection is removed. The telltale sign that a male cardinal feels threatened is the loud chirp it sounds. As danger nears the nest or nestlings, the chirping will become louder and quicker the closer the danger becomes.

There are many predators of the cardinal, including domestic or feral cats, falcons, hawks, shrikes, and some owls. The chicks fall prey to blue jays, snakes, squirrels and chipmunks.

Once prized as a pet, the cardinal now falls under the protection of the Migratory Bird Treaty Act of 1918 and can no longer be sold as a pet. By law, the cardinal cannot be killed, captured or possessed. Violators are subject to a heavy fine and up to six months in prison.

Hummingbirds

Figure 27. Ruby Throated Hummingbird

The hummingbird is the smallest of the birds that may visit your backyard. Their size is only a mere three to five inches. Hummingbirds have many unique features not found among any other species. They have the ability to hover in midair, they are the only bird that can fly backwards and their wings can flutter from twelve to eighty times per second. The "hummer" receives its name from the sound it makes from its beating wings. The sound has been described as similar to the sound of buzzing bees.

As pollinators, hummingbirds have a specialized diet. They rely on the nectar of flowers for their main food source. Small insects and spiders contribute proteins, vitamins and minerals to the hummer's diet. Hummingbirds, like bees, can distinguish flowers that produce high nectar content. They ignore flowering plants that produce less than ten percent sugar. The hummingbird is considered a pollinator of many flowering species including those that bees cannot fertilize. It is important to not use pesticides or fertilizers on flowers that hummingbirds, bees or butterflies will likely visit; their small and fragile sizes cannot stand the poisons absorbed into the flower and will eventually get sick and die.

Hummingbirds are also territorial, especially when regarding food. They will fight off other hummingbirds when they find a consistent food source. If you keep your hummingbird feeder full and maintain a balanced level of sugar to water, you will have a hummingbird that visits regularly. Hummingbirds usually feed on flowers that range from reds and oranges to bright pinks. Planting native flowers to your region that produce these colors will also draw hummingbirds to your garden. Some plants are developed specifically for hummingbirds though you must ensure their flowers produce colors in the red spectrum.

Hummingbirds are a migratory bird and will travel to Mexico or Central America during the winter months for warmth. Their normal range is from southern Alaska to Mexico; the highest concentration of hummingbirds can be found in Central America during the migratory season.

Hummingbirds are polygamous. After mating the male leaves while the female cares for the young. Mating is generally quick and males do not take part in nesting or chick raising. The nest size of the hummingbird can range from the size of a half of a walnut shell to several inches. Most of the nests are held together with spider web silk. Each nest holds two very small eggs, about the size of a grain of rice, and is incubated between 12 and 23 days. The mother feeds her young hatchlings arthropods and aphids as their main diet.

The hummingbird can sing but cannot sustain a note for long. Instead hummingbirds make sounds through their feathers. When courting, the male hummingbird will go into a steep dive, producing a chirping sound from their tail feathers. Most hummingbirds communicate through the sounds produced through short chirps and whistles.

The Robin

Figure 28. Robin

The robin is a common sight across all of North America. The robin can be seen early in the morning hopping around any lawn looking for earthworms and late in the afternoon searching for fruit and berries. With its orange breast and steel gray wings the robin is readily noticeable even to a novice bird watcher. During summer they are solitary in nature but in winter large flocks can be seen that consist of hundreds of robins. Robins are generally considered the harbinger of spring. Though you may not see them as much during winter months, they typically remain close to their territory.

During the fall and winter months robins eat only fruits and berries, as their chief spring and summer staple, earthworms, become inactive. It is recommended to provide robins with fruit trees that produce berries during the winter and to add fruits and berries to your platform bird feeder. Oranges and raisins are a favorite of robins. By providing robins with fruits from a platform feeder, you will begin to see them well into the winter months.

Robins have a unique habit many people find enthralling. During the winter, robins form roosts whose numbers can reach up to thousands of birds. When they take flight in unison, the observer may be fascinated by the way the entire flock moves together as one.

During summer, females rarely join roosts until nesting season ends after which they reunite with males. Younger robins normally feed by themselves until they reach maturity; only then will they take up residence with the other birds in the flock.

When watching robins feed you may notice their dietary habits. Robins will eat worms and other ground crawling insects in the mornings. In the afternoon they change to fruits and berries found in trees and tall shrubs. Thus it is important to add fruits, fruit bearing trees and shrubs to your yard as robins will flock to sample and eat these berries and fruits. By avoiding fertilizers or pesticides, you allow robins to dine on any insects in your lawn without risk of being poisoned.

The song of the robin is very familiar to most people who venture out during the early morning hours. They have a distinctive song of crisp whistles that is repeated until they take flight to feed. Their calls to each other are similar to a "chunk" sound and their alarm call is a "*yeep*" that increases in pitch as danger nears them.

Woodpeckers

There is no mistaking the sound of a woodpecker. They make a "rat-a-tat-tat" sound as they peck at a tree looking for food or clear out a nesting area. Woodpeckers can be found in wooded areas; however, if you have an area with mature trees you may have woodpeckers in and around your yard. Woodpeckers often frequent dead trees and stumps for bugs, so by keeping deadwood in your yard you will definitely attract woodpeckers.

Woodpeckers can be found almost anywhere in North America and across the entire globe. They feed and nest mainly in trees in the northeastern United States. Other species around the world have adapted to various other nesting areas such as dedicated woodpecker boxes, cacti and other assorted natural habitats.

Woodpeckers have a unique physical make up. They have four toes; two facing backwards and two facing forwards to aid in grabbing and staying vertical on trees and stumps. You will also notice that the woodpecker tail is stiff and straight. This is for balancing on tree trunks when insect hunting or boring out a nesting cavity.

In the Northeast, the main diet of the woodpecker is found in both live and dead trees. They will dig and chisel away at trees and other wood sources with their long, sharp beaks until they reach their food source. They then use their long, sticky tongues to reach the insects and feed inside. The woodpecker also uses its beak to poke out holes inside the trees to use as roosts and nesting areas.

Figure 29. Hairy Woodpecker

The hairy woodpecker is a common sight on the east coast of North America and can even be seen feeding from bird feeders that have sunflower or milo seeds. This medium sized woodpecker is a non-migratory bird, found in the region year round. They can be seen in the winter foraging through pine trees and forests and drinking sap that leaks from tree bark. They will sometimes gravitate towards a hummingbird feeder to feed on its sweet nectar.

The main food of the woodpecker is beetles and larva found in trees and dead wood. They also enjoy ants and moth larva. On occasion, they will eat bees, caterpillars, spiders, crickets and grasshoppers. If you supply a suet bird feeder, you will be able to see them up close and watch their entertaining eating patterns as they peck and lick the suet.

Finches and Sparrows

Finches and sparrows are quick, colorful little birds seen darting in and around your backyard in search of seeds to feed on. There are many different varieties but the most popular and often sighted ones in the Northeast are the American Goldfinch, the house finch, the grosbeak, the lark and chipping sparrows.

Figure 30. American Goldfinch

Finches and sparrows are seed eaters. They have strictly vegetarian diets and will frequent bird feeders put out by humans. Finches and sparrows are flock birds, usually flying in groups of ten to a few hundred, especially during the winter months. They tend to remain within an area; species in the Northeast will usually remain even throughout the winter months. Although finches do not follow a specific migration pattern, if the winter temperature drops to subzero temperatures they will fly southward to warmer weather.

Favorite wild foods of finches and sparrows are the thistle plant, the nyjer and the aster. During the winter months you can expect to see these little birds more frequently at your bird feeders. It doesn't matter if it is a hopper style, tube style, or platform feeder. Finches will feed on the ground as well as in feeders as long as there is a food supply. A word of advice: finches and sparrows can be 'messy' feeder eaters so be sure to keep the ground clean to prevent unwanted bacterial growth from seeds that remain uneaten.

The nests of the finches and sparrows are normally built in medium to tall shrubs. The female is the primary nest builder while the male brings material to the female. The nests are built in a more exposed area compared to other birds though they do not fall to predation as often since they nest later than other species. After thistles have gone to seed, the finches will then nest, usually in mid to late summer.

The songs of the finches and many sparrows are a series of tweets and warbles. They will repeat the pattern continuously with the males singing to the females well before mating season. These calls have been compared to someone murmuring "*po-ta-to chip*" in very soft tones while a danger call is a very loud "*bay-bee*" sound.

If you want more finches to visit your yard, plant thistle, nyjer and milkweed plants. In the bird feeder, sunflower and nyjer seeds will attract finches and sparrows. If you keep your feeder full you will be rewarded with many visits, with some returning daily.

The Chickadee

Figure 31. Chickadee

One of the most beloved of all songbirds, the little chickadee is a sight to watch as they perform their antics. Their curious nature is reminiscent of a child. Although not recommended, the chickadee is one of the few wild birds that can be fed from human hands. The chickadee can be found anywhere in the continental United States and in wooded, urban and rural areas.

The chickadee is a non-migratory bird except in extreme northern regions when temperatures dip well below freezing. When chickadees do migrate, they form large flocks for protection from predators and to more easily locate food sources. When observing a chickadee flock, look carefully inside the group as there are often other larger birds. These birds are not hunting chickadees but working with them in search for food.

Chickadees will call out when a food source is located, which forms a certain cohesion within the group. Chickadees also have a sort of primitive social structure among their flocks. They establish a hierarchy which keeps the group driven for the purpose of hunting food and protection. The males form the upper part of the ladder, females are next while older chickadees will fall between the females and the younger chickadees.

The chickadee has a short two-whistle sound for its song and is constantly singing to keep in contact with others nearby. Their songs have evolved over time to adapt to the changes wrought by urbanization and can contain up to thirteen different versions of the two-tone whistle. An interesting tidbit is that the chickadee received its name from its song. It makes a distinct "chick-a-dee-dee" sound. Their "dee-dee" call is also an indicator of perceived threat levels -- the frequency and loudness of the "dee-dee" increases as the threat nears.

The diet of the chickadee consists of mainly insects, especially caterpillars, during the summer season. During winter months, the chickadees' diet changes from insects to mostly seeds as insects become a smaller part of their diet. You can help the chickadee by adding suet, peanuts, and mealworms to your platform or hopper feeder while keeping sunflower and milo seeds in your tube feeders. Another favorite of the chickadee is peanut butter. You can spread this on a ledge or a cardboard paper towel roll. This will ensure that the chickadees that frequent your yard will receive a balanced and nutritious diet during the winter months.

The Blue Jay

Figure 32. Blue Jaye

The blue jay is a very common visitor to most backyards. Located throughout the eastern United States they range from southern Minnesota to the eastern part of Texas and all along the east coast. Blue jays are territorial and you will normally have the same blue jays in your yard year round. Their lifespan is among the longest of wild birds of their size, with the oldest recorded age being 17 years in the wild.

The blue jay is not considered a migratory bird; only the northernmost birds migrate to the south for warmer climates during the harsh winters. While the blue jays' migratory patterns have been researched, no direct pattern has been determined. Some birds will stay in an area year round while some will migrate every other year.

Blue jays are known to be loud and noisy, highly intelligent, extremely bold and very aggressive. They will not hesitate to chase down a hawk or owl that has entered into their territory. They also have been known to dive at humans if they feel threatened or consider their nest at risk. Other birds, especially smaller ones, tend to feed with the blue jay because they make loud, shrill warning cries when they sense a predator approaching. Smaller birds take advantage of the blue jay's tendency to chase away a predator, regardless of its size. It also allows smaller birds to take flight before predators reach them.

A blue jays diet varies widely. They will eat nuts, acorns, seeds, weed seeds, meat, peanuts, berries, bread, snails, table scraps, and on very rare occasions, eggs. Since their black bills are extremely hard, they find it easy to crack open nuts and acorns which are among their favorite foods. A suet feeder in your back yard will attract blue jay visitors. They mate for life and will remain together until one dies. They both build the nest together and share in the rearing of hatchlings.

While the blue jay prefers evergreens, they will nest just about anywhere. A female blue jay will lay between 4 to 5 eggs. The female will incubate them with the male bringing food to her. The young will begin to fledge (leave the nest) between 7 and 10 days. The fledglings will stay with the parents until the onset of winter when they will go on their own to reduce the competition for food.

The blue jays songs are as varied as its diet. A blue jay can mimic a human's speech if heard often enough. It will make loud screeching calls and is often heard mimicking hawks to locate them. Blue jays will also sound an alarm cry that calls together jays in the area to mob hawks and owls that stray too close to the jays' nests.

The Bluebird

Figure 33. Male and Female Eastern Blue Bird

The Eastern bluebird, a medium sized bird, can be seen during the summer months chasing insects and looking for suitable nesting for his mate of choice. The Eastern bluebird is a handsome bird with royal blue and rose colors that make them easy to distinguish.

A female bluebird's colors are similar to that of the male except that the females' colors are slightly lighter. The female is the nest builder and raises the young brood as the male's only job is to bring nesting materials for the female.

The bluebird is a favorite of many gardeners since this bird has a voracious appetite for bugs. They will quickly rid a garden of insects. Bluebirds are particularly fond of ground and low flying pests such as moths, mosquitoes and ants.

Bluebirds suffered a rapid decline in population due to competition with European starlings and house sparrows, both invasive, non-native species. By providing a safe nesting haven for the bluebirds that visit your yard, you will be contributing to their resurgence.

Bluebirds can spot their prey from over sixty feet away and will make long slow sweeping flights to capture their prey. Besides insects, bluebirds are known to hunt small snakes, salamanders and lizards. An additional part of their diet besides insects includes berries such as honeysuckle, mistletoe, sumac and black cherries.

The habitat of the Eastern Bluebird is wide-open fields surrounded by trees. There should be little ground cover as the bluebird hunts on the ground for insects -- ground cover hides their prey. With recent efforts to rebuild the bluebird population, their presence is noticed more often by open pastures and fields, parks and golf courses.

The bluebird songs are a series of short warbles with an occasional chattering mixed in. The song is sung by the males to attract females to their nest selection. Paired males will sing a similar version but with a much softer tone while the female is laying eggs.

The call of the bluebird is generally a soft pitched "tu-a-wee" sound. The bluebird uses this song as a way of communicating with other bluebirds to stay in contact. Bluebirds also use this call to alert the nestlings that they are approaching the nest with food. Similarly, when the bluebird feels threatened, they will make a "chit-chit-chit" sound. Another sound the bluebird makes when facing danger is a loud clack as they shut their beaks hard before diving at a predator.

Having a feeder will not often attract bluebirds but nesting boxes placed correctly will bring them to your backyard, provided trees surround the yard. You can spot bluebirds sitting on power lines and fences searching for their favorite prey -- insects -- especially near open fields and meadows.

The Purple Martin

Figure 34. Purple Martins Male and Female

The purple martin is a migratory bird that spends its winters in Brazil and migrates to the Northeast to nest and mate during the spring and summer months. The purple martin is a member of the swallow family and is the largest member of that species. They grow to around seven and a half inches and can weigh up to two ounces. There are three distinct species recognized in the purple martin family, depending on the region where they breed. The one we mention here is the ***Progne subis subis***, which breeds in the northeastern United States and relies on humans to supply their nesting needs.

Purple martins are monogamous and spend their adult lives with their mate. The mating pair builds their nest and feeds the hatchlings together continuously until the fledglings are ready to leave the nest and venture out on their own. During this time, the adults will train and continue to feed the fledglings together. In about two weeks, the fledgling will leave their parents but can sometimes be seen returning to the fabricated house to rest and sleep.

After the introduction of European starlings and house wrens to North America in the 1980s, the purple martin population began a steep decline. Backyard birders noticed that where once there were thousands of martins nesting, there were now only hundreds. Thanks to their intervention in the Northeast, backyard birders have made great strides in helping this species regain its once populous status.

To accomplish this goal, backyard birders need to provide proper nesting for the martins and follow a regimented cleaning and care of their houses. This is when the journal you've been keeping will become invaluable. Purple martins send 'scouts' ahead to find nesting area. If you have kept up your journal from prior years, you will have a general idea when to expect them. This is the time to make sure the houses are clean, free from predators and competition and positioned appropriately.

The sounds, songs and calls of the purple martin are said to be an assortment of rattles, croaks and chortles. The purple martin's songs are rich, throaty and loud. There are distinct songs that the purple martin makes. One call is for courtship, one for the morning call and another that announces the end of the season. After you have set up your martin houses, you can invest in a purple martin audio tape that will play the songs of the martin, luring them into your backyard and nesting site.

14. Specific Plants for Bird Gardens

Below is a list of fauna and flora specific to each species. The F equals a food source, while the S equals a shade source.

BIRD	Ash	Birch	Cedar(red)/juniper	Cotoneaster	Crab Apple	Dogwood	Elderberry	Holly	Maple	Oak	Pine	Rose	Spruce	Sumac
Blue jay	F/S	F			F	F/S	F/S	F/S		F	F			F
Bunting							F/S							
Cardinal										F		F/S		
Catbird				F	F/S	F/S	F/S	F/S					F	
Cedar waxwing	F/S	F		F	F/S	F/S	F/S	F/S	F/S	F	F	F	F/S	
Chickadee	F/S	F/S	F/S			F/S	F/S	F/S		F	F	F	F/S	F
Cowbird			F/S								F/S		F/S	
Crossbill		F/S	F/S								F/S		F/S	
Duck	F									F/S	F/S			
Finch	F/S	F	F/S	F	F/S	F/S	F/S	F/S	F/S	F	F	F		
Flicker			F/S		F/S	F/S	F/S	F/S			F			F
Goldfinch		F			F							F	F/S	
Goose											S		F/S	
Grackle			F/S											S
Grosbeak	F/S				F/S	F/S	F/S		F/S		F	F	F/S	
Junco		F				F/S					F			
Mockingbird			F/S	F	F/S		F/S	F/S		F	S	F	F/S	F
Mourning dove		F					F/S	F/S		F	F		F/S	
Nuthatch							F/S	F/S		F			F/S	
Oriole					F	F/S				F			F/S	

BIRD	Ash	Birch	Cedar(red)/juniper	Cotoneaster	Crab Apple	Dogwood	Elderberry	Holly	Maple	Oak	Pine	Rose	Spruce	Sumac
Pheasant	F/S													F/S
Pine siskin		F							F/S		F		F/S	
Redpoll		S											F/S	
Sparrow						F/S	F/S		F/S		F	S	F/S	F
Starling														
Tanager						F/S		F/S		S			F/S	F
Thraser				F			F/S	F/S		F	F			F
Thrush			F/S			F/S	F/S			F	F	F		F
Titmouse		F			F		F/S	F/S		F	F			
Towhee		F			F		F/S	F/S		F	F	S		F
Warbler			F/S		F		F/S	F/S	F/S		F			F
Woodpecker					F/S	F/S	F/S	F/S		F	F		F/S	F

From the 'Old Farmer's Almanac'

15. Seed List for Specific Birds

Courtesy of Wild-bird-watching.com

When choosing birdseed to place in your bird feeding station, determine the types of birds you want to attract. Try setting out several varieties and be sure to include a source of water during both summer and winter. Below is a list of seeds for birds that frequent the northeastern part of the United States.

When providing seed and food for the birds in your yard, you will see that many species enjoy the

same type of seed. Most birds enjoy fruits such as apples and oranges as well as raisins. Though this is just a sampling of birds that visit the Northeast, these are the main visitors and much of what they enjoy is shared by others with similar tastes.

- **Blue Jays** -- sunflower seed, safflower, cracked corn, peanuts, suet, bread, peanut butter, lard mixes and seed mixes

- **House Finches and Gold Finches** -- Mixed seed, peanuts, fruit, suet, nyjer, sunflower, safflower, thistle, hulled sunflower, millet, fruit.

- **Orioles** -- oranges, apples, grape jelly, oriole jelly, sugar water, soft raisins

Figure 35. Oriole Eating Jelly

- **Painted Buntings** -- sunflower seeds, seed mix.

Figure 36. Painted Bunting

- **Red winged Blackbirds** -- suet, bread, cracked corn, mixed seeds, sunflower seeds, millet, sunflower chips.

- **Robins, Bluebirds and Thrushes** -- Apples, sunflower seeds, bread, grapes, suet, mealworms, berries, raisins, nut meal, seed mixes.

- **Cardinals** -- Cracked corn, nuts, sunflower seeds, safflower, millet, peanuts, apples, bread.

- **Black-capped Chickadees** -- Sunflower seeds, peanuts, bread, suet

- **Downey Woodpeckers** -- Sunflower seeds, corn, cornbread, peanut butter, suet, shelled peanuts, sunflower seeds.

- **Grosbeaks and Buntings** -- Sunflower seeds, safflower apples, fruit, suet, millet, bread, peanut kernels.

Figure 37. Grosbeak

- **Titmouse** -- Sunflower seeds, suet, bread, safflower, peanuts, peanut kernels.

- **Mockingbirds and Thrashers** -- Halved apples, fruit, bread, suet, sunflower seeds, nuts

Figure 38. Mockingbird

- **Waxwings** -- Berries, raisins, sliced apple, canned peas, currants, grapes.

- **Quail** -- Cracked corn, millet, berries

- **Doves** - cracked corn, sunflower seeds, milo, bread, nyjer, nuts

16. Backyard Bird Log

A backyard bird journal can be made from any notebook or even a simple spreadsheet on your laptop. Some items you may want to list in your journal include:

- Date and Time
- Gender
- Location of bird sighting
- Number of birds seen
- Behavior observations
- Habitat description
- General weather conditions
- Bird sounds
- Type of Bird and species
- Sketches or photographs of things you see or of the birds

I have found that using a notepad works well so it is always handy when I am bird watching.

Others will carry a journal type book complete with photos. It's just a matter of how in-depth you want to get into your bird watching in your backyard. By keeping a journal, you become more than just an observer of the birds that visit. You move into participation and your journal will grow over the years.

After a while, you will begin to notice some birds that are regular visitors. Not just a certain species, but a particular bird. For example, in my journal I've noted that five birds visit me regularly and each one appears at almost a set period every time.

It is exciting to see the same birds year after year and welcome a friend back to the yard.

17. Recommended Resources

Newsletter

Sign up to AttractingWildBirds.com to get strategies on attracting wild birds to your backyard, creating an organic and edible garden and much more!

Go to http://www.attractingwildbirds.com to join us at Attracting Wild Birds

Figure 39. Long Tailed Titmouse

www.ingramcontent.com/pod-product-compliance
Lightning Source LLC
Chambersburg PA
CBHW050807290526
45792CB00001B/22